Vintage Barnes and Mortlake

Researched and compiled by the Barnes and Mortlake History Society

Front cover: Only the forge with house and outbuildings survive from Mortlake High Street as depicted here in the 1880s. All on the right lies under the highway. The backyards of Falla's (established by Myler Falla in 1855) and the butcher's (there in 1811) contain The Charlie Butler, opened in 1968. The lady in black walks under a gasolier inscribed Gospel Hall, where workmen were weaned away from pubs. The Old George and The Two Brewers were handy and the signs are prominent. The ventilating cone just beyond Bulls Alley belongs to a waterside malthouse.

Published by Hendon Publishing Co., Ltd., Hendon Mill, Nelson, Lancs.

© Barnes and Mortlake History Society, 1979.

Printed by Turner & Earnshaw Ltd., Sycamore Avenue, Burnley, Lancs.

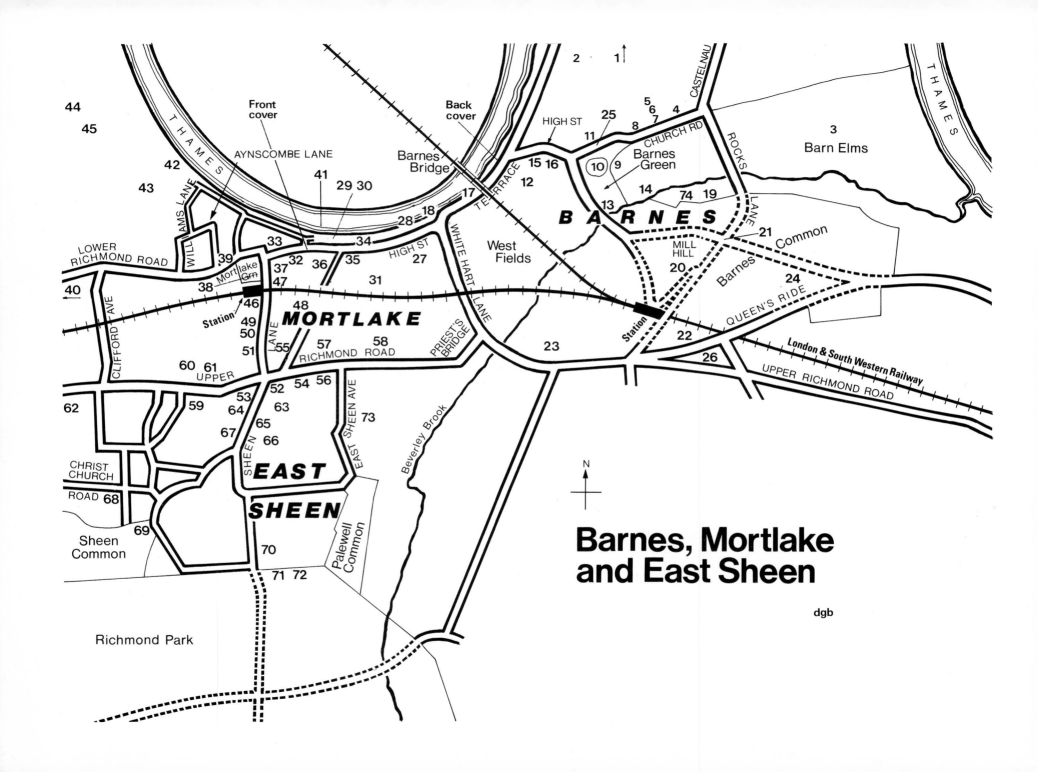

Barnes, Mortlake and East Sheen

Introduction

The appearance of **Barnes and Mortlake as it was** two years ago aroused great interest from residents and friends of our area. Many have written to us, sharing their nostalgic memories, providing us with important information and pointing out a few minor errors! In preparing this complementary volume, we have varied the material as far as possible and have been able to include a number of photographs which have only recently come to light. Although we have kept to the format of a feasible visual tour which can be undertaken with the help of the map, **Vintage Barnes and Mortlake** is perhaps more in the nature of an anthology than its companion. We hope that both books will give pleasure separately or together.

The area is confined to the old parishes of Barnes and Mortlake, and once again, the difference in character between the two former villages should be stressed. We have some idea of their appearance in the late eighteenth and early nineteenth centuries from the many wash drawings by such artists as Hieronymous Grimm, John Hassell and Edward Hassell. Their work is evidently more accurate than the few early prints, which are of course far more widely known, and many details in the drawings can be confirmed from early photographs. This link provides us with a visual survey up to the present day.

In spite of the abundance of surviving photographs, a number of vanished buildings and views appear to be unrecorded and this confirms the documentary value of what we do have and the need to bring it to a wider public to study and enjoy. Many of these pictures are filled with fascinating details which amply reward their careful scrutiny with a magnifying glass. As before, they range in date from mid-Victorian times until just before the last war with the majority originating in the two decades bordering the turn of the century. Local characters and shops are well represented as well as important events in recent local history.

Our surroundings constantly change. Since **Barnes and Mortlake as it was** came out, Nash's shop, photographed in about 1860, has been demolished and Barnes Parish Church gutted by fire. It is tragic that no complete photographic record of the church monuments seems to exist which will make reconstruction of many of them an impossibility. On the other hand, admirable photographs were taken of the many old buildings demolished before the recent widening of Mortlake High Street which should provide rich pickings for our potential successors when they bring out **their** book in, say, fifty years time.

The photographs have been selected by the same team from the Barnes and Mortlake History Society, Maisie Brown, Caroline Crimp, Raymond Gill, Mary Grimwade and Charles Hailstone; the captions have been written by Caroline Crimp, Mary Grimwade, Charles Hailstone and Bernard Sanders. The photographic material has been loaned by the Richmond-upon-Thames Central Library, Mortlake Parish Church and the United Reformed Church, East Sheen, as well as the private collections of Mr. C. Bailey, Mr. Leslie Freeman, Mr. Raymond Gill, Miss Mary Grimwade, Mr. Charles Hailstone, Mrs. A. Harbord, Mr. Richard Levin, Mrs. Margaret Macdonald. Mr. Leslie Paton, Mrs. R. Pattullo, Miss E. Phillips, the late Mr. J. Seal and Mr. F. T. P. Windsor (who, incidentally, designed the Charter Day and 1937 Coronation decorations). It is a pleasure and a privilege to be able to use material from so many different sources and we are most grateful to all of them for their kind permission to reproduce it here. The map is based on the one designed for us by Peter Taylor. Richard Jeffree, *Chairman of the Barnes and Mortlake History Society.*

THE TERRACE, BARNES.

BARNES

2.   **Below:** Here a family group celebrate Queen Victoria's Diamond Jubilee. This delightful photograph shows Walnut Tree Farmhouse which stood back from Lonsdale Road and was demolished in the 1920s when the Lowther Estate was developed. The farm lands are now covered by Barnes Sports Club, Lowther, Suffolk and neighbouring roads. A little remains open to the public as Suffolk Road recreation ground.

1.   **Above:** In 1910 this little girl stood on the stile, beside the track which led up what is now Kilmington Road to the Bessant's house, Lonsdale Farm. Baynes House now occupies the site and the Castelnau estate covers the market gardens once intensively cultivated by the family who occupied that homestead.

3.   **Right**: Polo at Ranelagh on the old polo
ground south-east of Barn Elms House. Much
thought was given to the building of the original
polo pavilion. The spectators had their backs to
the setting sun and were shielded from the
elements by the covered verandah and balcony.
A dining room and refreshment room were on
ground floor level and adequate changing
accomodation even included a masseur's room.
An open, but covered, pony shed was provided
at the rear while the umpire sat aloft over all in
his covered box.

4.   **Right**: Byfield House, Barnes. The north
view of the house in Church Road which was
originally two dwellings built in the 1690s and
joined together between 1798 and 1800. It
became a boys' school in 1828 and the owner,
on acquiring more land, was allowed to enclose
part of the ancient path leading from Church
Road to the river which accounts for the bend
at the southern end of Ferry Road leading to
Castelnau. The house was demolished in 1902
and Byfield Hall now stands on the site.

5. **Above:** The exterior, east view of St. Mary's, Barnes, c.1877. At this time the south aisle contained the only altar and the northern section was an extension for seating only, erected in 1852 at a cost of £1,972. The stables of the Homestead, now Homestead Cottage, stand north of the church path.

6.   **Left:** The interior of St. Mary's sometime between 1906 and 1911 after the new sanctuary and chancel had been added. The floral decorations are placed in readiness for the Dedication Festival in June and the appropriate hymn numbers appear on the board. It was not until 1911 that electric lighting was installed at a cost of £160, and two years later the chancel screen was erected in memory of Hilda Jacobsen. The pulpit was new but the candle bracket and book rest were of older date.

7.   **Right:** On 5th May 1933 St. Mary's bells were taken down for rehanging. The oldest is dated 1575 and was cast by order of Thomas Smythe, the second made by William Land 1616, and the third by William Eldridge 1667. To commemorate Queen Victoria's Diamond Jubilee the peal was made up to eight, while a ninth, the clock and sanctus bell, bears the inscription H.N. 16Ɛ7 (sic).

Here the Rev. F.H.E. Harfitt, curate from 1932 to 1936, stands with Mr. Geoffrey Dearmer and workmen outside the Homestead when the bells were down from the tower.

8. Right: This early photograph of Barnes Green showing Church Row in 1860 is of unusual interest. The pathway on the right led to the pond and the outbuildings on the extreme left were in the garden of Frog Hall, demolished in 1911. Of these eight cottages five may still be identified as the shops nos. 77-85 Church Road.

9. Right: Barnes Green School. c. 1890. A group of Victorian schoolgirls and infants stand outside the school with their mistress. From 1883 onwards three other schools had opened for local pupils namely Westfields Boys, Westfields Girls and Infants and Castelnau Girls and Infants. In September 1903 a separate school was opened at Westfields for infants only. This is the only one now left functioning on its original site.

10.   Above: Barnes Pond c.1900. Paddling and fishing for tiddlers has been a delightful occupation for Barnes children throughout the decades. The pond also offered a few restful moments for cart-horses who were able to enter the water down the prepared slope which can be seen in the left hand corner of this photograph. The boy, happily leaning on his home-made cart, contentedly watches his group of school-fellows.

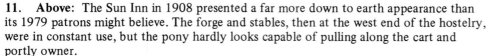

11.   **Above:** The Sun Inn in 1908 presented a far more down to earth appearance than its 1979 patrons might believe. The forge and stables, then at the west end of the hostelry, were in constant use, but the pony hardly looks capable of pulling along the cart and portly owner.

12.   **Above Right:** This attractive letter box originally stood in Cleveland Road. It has now been replaced by one bearing the letters ER II. Such boxes are often helpful in tracing building development of roads and housing estates. There are still others in the area of Victorian origin, and a rare Edward VIII one stands at the corner of West Temple Sheen and Temple Sheen Road.

13. **Left**: A family group stands outside Cleveland Cottage in Station Road. Despite the obviously best clothes a treasured skipping rope and ball are recorded and the pet dog occupies as prominent a place as the elegantly dressed baby. Cleveland Cottage was demolished in the late 1920s and the site is now covered by the ancillary buildings of the Methodist Church.

14. **Right**: The boys of Beverley School, clad in white flannels, are enjoying a game of tennis in the school grounds. Mr. Corelli Stevens moved his school there from Beverley Road in 1896 and remained until his retirement about 1930. The house, built in 1705, was originally named The Laurels and had had a number of notable residents before being demolished shortly after Mr. Stevens departure. The Crescent and Beverley Close now cover the site of the house and one time extensive grounds.

15.   **Above:** J. Seal, Purveyor of meat had every reason to be proud of the royal coat of arms. Although his shop would be condemned today for unhygienic reasons it obviously supplied meat of high quality to the upper class Barnes society. Shoppers who are familiar with Barnes High Street now will recognise this corner shop as one belonging to a supermarket chain but the butcher's shop alongside still trades under the name of Seal.

16. **Below:** How delightful to have one's meat delivered by this spanking little pony and cart. Presumably it made numerous journeys to take large joints to the residents of White Lodge, Richmond Park.

17. **Above Right:** Barnes Terrace, before the first river wall was built, was very frequently flooded. Here, however, on a fine summer's day at the turn of the century, pleasure craft can be observed and the boat house on the Chiswick bank is doing considerable business. At this time Duke's Meadows were not laid out on the east side of the bridge. The little girl in her straw hat, button boots and starched pinafore pauses to enjoy the scene along with a member of the police force.

18. **Right:** The White Hart may not have altered greatly since 1900 but the road traffic certainly has. No longer are No. 9 buses horse drawn. Marsham Lodge, west of the hostelry, was demolished for road widening in 1930 and youth club premises built on its site. As the boundary between Barnes and Mortlake runs along the centre of White Hart Lane this photograph shows the first and last houses of both parishes.

19. **Above:** This rustic bridge crossed a small tributary of Beverley Brook which rose on the common opposite to Elm Grove Road and flowed into the brook near the end of Glebe Road. This watercourse is clearly shown on early maps of the area. The water from this spring was reputed to be very pure. The bridge took pedestrians across the stream from Rectory Road on to the common. Although this arm of the brook is now dried up it can be traced running parallel to Ranelagh Avenue.

20. **Above Right:** Mill Hill, Barnes Common. c.1900. The common contained many sandy places, like the one shown here, until well into the 1930s. They were the delight of many generations of children who came with bucket and spade and played happily on summer afternoons eating a picnic tea on a seat close at hand.

21. **Right:** At the turn of the century the cross roads on Barnes Common used to be a quiet place to rest and chat to acquaintances. Plenty of seating accomodation was provided which would hardly be appreciated today when the constantly changing traffic lights result in fumes and the noise of car engines. At this date there was still a slip road making a triangular island of this juncture.

22.   **Above:** This old L.S.W.R. engine of 1883 is
shunting in the goods yard at Barnes Station. It ran
regularly from Feltham to Barnes via Hounslow
delivering and picking up freight. Here, on an
October day, the coal trucks were laden with a
winter fuel supply for local residents. The engine
was scrapped in 1959 after a life time's service.
The goods yard has now been closed for some while
and its future use has become a matter of
considerable concern.

23.   **Right:** Here, about 1920, are the workers of
Mr. Walter Barker's market garden setting forth on
their annual outing. Mr. Barker farmed land between
the two level crossings, now the Vine Road recreation
ground, as well as other areas in the neighbourhood.
He lived in Tangier Lodge, Vine Road, one of the
houses shown here in this photograph.

26.   **Below**: The Manor House Hotel was demolished in 1961 and a block of luxury flats now stands on the site. This house, built in 1778, was the Barnes Workhouse until 1836 and the original grounds were bounded by Queen's Ride, Upper Richmond Road and the parish boundary with Putney, in all 23 acres. The architect was Kenton Couse who was just building Richmond Bridge. The Workhouse cost £777 to erect. By 1837 it was privately let and had been renamed the Manor House.

24, 25.   **Above**: Here the Lord Lieutenant of Surrey is presenting the Charter to incorporate the Borough of Barnes to J. D. Firmston Esq. J.P., the Charter Mayor. Before him lies the mace which was his personal gift to the Borough together with the Mayoral chains of office. The ceremony took place in a marquee erected on the common immediately over the Putney boundary and almost opposite the old gate house. (see *No. 25 Barnes and Mortlake As It Was*). The first meeting of the newly elected Town Council was held at noon on 9th November 1932.

Left.
After the formal presentation and speeches there followed a procession around the new Borough in which scenes from local history were depicted. Here, between Pond and Sun Inn, Queen Elizabeth I rides by to commemorate her visits to Barn Elms. In the further distance the first boat race crew represents the earliest row from Putney to Mortlake in 1845. Incorporated in the Borough's coat-of-arms were a light and dark blue oar.

MORTLAKE

27.   **Left**: Riverside Mortlake about 1927. The Beverley Brook relief culvert was in construction under White Hart Lane and the caisson work and piling is seen in the top right corner. Barnes Urban District Council's electricity station with its fine chimney, demolished in 1964, opened in May 1901, supplying the country's cheapest current. An electric luffing crane on rails unloads coal from a barge near the chimney's shadow. No motors are to be seen and there are allotments on the Ashleigh House site. The Limes, then the seat of local government and called the Council House, reveals its grand proportions.

28.   **Right**: Charter Day at Mortlake. Having fun with the Princess Amelia fire engine of 1758 on Charter Day, 1932, in the Council depot.

MORTLAKE TAPESTRY HOUSE

IN THIS BUILDING
WAS CARRIED ON THE FAMOUS TAPESTRY MANUFACTURE
WHICH WAS INTRODUCED INTO ENGLAND
AND ESTABLISHED HERE ABOUT THE YEAR 1619
BY SIR FRANCIS CRANE KNIGHT,
UNDER THE PATRONAGE OF KING JAMES I.
IT WAS CONTINUED DURING THE REIGN OF KING CHARLES L
WHO ACQUIRED THE PROPERTY
AND BOUGHT THE CELEBRATED CARTOONS OF RAPHAEL
IN ORDER TO BE COPIED HERE.

RESTORED 1877.

29, 30. Left & Above: Mortlake Tapestry Works. As the tablet shows, the tapestry works were established in 1619 and within a few years were world famous. This building, known locally as the Lower Dutch House, had looms on the first floor, more looms and a designer's room on the top floor, and at ground level living accommodation for the weavers. A smaller building, known as the upper Dutch House, later became a dwelling house and is the original part of 119 Mortlake High Street, formerly known as Suthrey House.

31. Right: The quiet backs of old Mortlake High Street. It is Monday washday and the Worple Street clothes-lines are full. The bus garage, right of Tinderbox Alley, opened with six horse buses in 1901 and the brickwork looks new. More washing is discerned in the close huddle of cottages now Avondale House and Montgomery House flats. The white house with a walled orchard is Thames House, now Kindell House flats. The square tower of the parish church with its satisfying cupola gives an essentially Mortlakey atmosphere. Ripley Gardens replaced the allotments around 1927.

32. Left: Mortlake High Street looking west in 1865. This is one of the earliest photographs of the High Street as it looked over one hundred years ago. Fields, the drapers, appears to have a large assortment of goods on display and a delivery cart is pulled up almost alongside. The unswept and rough appearance of the road must have caused considerable trouble to the ladies whose long skirts were constantly trailing in mud or dust.

33. Above right: Mortlake Tithe Barn (Rear view). This building stood at the west end of Mortlake High Street on the north side. In 1783 it was discovered that the people of Mortlake had not been giving tithes and there was a great dispute concerning this. Even tithes of private garden produce were demanded. The only exemptions were horses used for husbandry in the parish, cows milked in the parish, sheep yielding wool in the parish, and cattle fed upon lands that had yielded hay or corn in the parish.

34. **Below:** Mortlake High Street. Old malt houses, most likely at the west end and on the north side of the street where most buildings connected with the brewing industry were grouped together. There was one malt house at the east end of the street, opposite the church, built in the late eighteenth century by John Prior who already had a malthouse at the east end. This second building was erected without permission on charity land leased from the parish.

35. **Left:** Mortlake High Street. Mr. and Mrs. Grayson at the door of their shop. This house, which was parish property, stood close to the church gates and had various uses over the years. At one time the cellar was the parish lock-up and on one of the walls was scratched a 'Peeler', a top-hatted policeman named after Sir Robert Peel, the founder of the police force in 1829. The house was demolished when the High Street was widened.

36. Above: Empire Day, 24th May 1909, at the National schools in Mullins Path, Mortlake. Together with Ascension Day this was a most important event in the school calendar and the sun always seemed to shine on the pageant enacted by the scholars. It was also used for linking Mortlake, England, with Mortlake, New South Wales, Australia, from whence came the flag on the mast. Headmaster Leaney, white haired and holding a hat stands on the right of the dais. On the extreme left beyond Church Path is Scarborough Lodge, long since gone.

37. **Left**: The 2nd Mortlake Boy Scouts, formed in 1919, parading outside the HQ in Alder Road, in 1923. Scoutmaster A. H. Marsh, unmistakable with white lanyard and moustache, stands left of the front rank and the chaplain from Mortlake parish church further down the road. The building material stacked beside Institute Cottages is for the HQ of the 1st Mortlake Sea Scouts who moved into it from Little St. Leonards the same year. Note the asphalt sidewalks, also Wainwright's Forge and Meadow View Cottages, now the Post Office sorting office and Allnat House.

38. **Left**: Lower Sheen Lane and Mortlake Green in 1906. Workmen rest beneath the shade of the great trees which bordered the Green, scene of fairs and religious meetings. For years it was tended by a greenkeeper in hard hat and gaiters, with besom broom. The mansard roofs belong to earlier times. The gabled parade remains, also The Railway Tavern, house of Meyer Rothenberg, poor rate collector in Napoleonic times. It became a pub after the railway came, hence its sign. The nearby dining rooms like many more was a boon to brewery workmen.

39. Right: Old houses between The Jolly Milkman and Waldeck Terrace before the Great War. The pub is partly seen on the left. As the painted notice on the wall of the cobbled yard announces, The Jolly Milkman took in guests, but seemingly no one above the station of 'commercials' or the passing cyclist. Hot dinners were served from midday until two o'clock: Beef Steak Pudding and two Veg 6d. (2½p), Cut from Joint and two Veg 6d, and Chops and Steaks, Tea and Coffee. Putney Hippodrome has a poster. It is August and Lew Lake is top of the bill.

40. Right: The original Beehive pub, probably a converted farmhouse, in a lonely stretch of the Lower Richmond Road near the edge of Mortlake. Black barns stand behind it. There are two signs, one an old-style beehive on top of a pole. Its customers came mostly from the surrounding market gardens. Supporting the neat picket fence are two in peaked caps, maybe from the gasworks not far from the pub and the dapper gent with watch-chain holds an openwork sack of produce. The picture was taken in March 1909.

41. **Above**: The Thames, Mortlake. A barge at Eastwood's wharf early in this century. The late Henry R. Morrissey of Barnes recorded that cement, lime, bricks and timber were delivered to Eastwood's and dock labourers came to Mortlake to unload. They were paid at 'piece' rates and, working very hard, they each earned about 12/- a day, a high sum for those times. They did not have a meal break but, whenever they wanted it, took bread, cheese and beer laid out for them.

42. **Above**: Derrick steam cranes minister over the building of Chiswick Bridge in July 1931. On the Mortlake side a light railway took spoil to Chalkers Corner. Some 45,000 tons of concrete utilising 6,000 tons of Portland cement, 3,400 tons of stone and 750 tons of steel were used in the structure. Sir Herbert Baker was the architect and it cost £208,284. The Prince of Wales (the late Duke of Windsor) opened it on Monday 3rd July 1933, as one of the noblest structures on the Thames. Note the chimney of the vanished Mortlake dust destruction works in the left distance.

43. Right: The last part of Mortlake to abandon its rurality lay between Chalkers Corner and Kew Meadows Path. Here was Pink's Farm in 1931, named from a Victorian market gardener. But the cold frames and the quaint old brick and timber farmhouse, red tiled and whitewashed, with its trees and fields were soon to disappear with the coming of Chiswick Bridge, which many thought should be called Mortlake Bridge, and its approach works. Happily the site is still used for nurseries on the western side of the bridge.

44. Below: West Park Avenue was laid out in the mid-1920s over the grounds of West Park, seen in this picture taken during the earlier years of the residence there of Dr. Miles Beale, the top-hatted figure standing with the ladies by the garden urns. This was an outlying part of the old parish of Mortlake, with a few bigger houses occupied by the gentry for whom a carriage and pair were essential. West Park was at one time the manor house of the Manor of East Sheen and Westhall.

45. **Above:** West Hall, Mortlake Road. This early eighteenth century house was part of the Manor of East Sheen and West Hall, a subsidiary manor since the reign of Henry VII. The Courts Baron of this small manor were held at 'The Rose Garden', a large house on the south side of the west end of Mortlake High Street. One side of West Hall was in the Manor of East Sheen and West Hall, the other in the Manor of Mortlake.

46. Left: Christmas time 1896 at W. H. Smith & Son's bookstall on Mortlake railway station. The gentleman with conspicuous watch-chain is presumably the manager, with hand firmly upon the well stocked front counter. Christmas numbers abound, among them The Sphere, Pall Mall Magazine and Pears. There is a profusion of novels, Nelson's Sixpenny Classics, newspapers, cards of pencils and pens and many other things to while away passengers' time between trains. Note the brick platform facings.

47. Left: The Sheen Lane level crossing has done more than anything else to give Mortlake a bad name. It has been Mortlake's misfortune ever since 1846 when the railway came here. Observe the semaphore signal post with ladder to get to the oil lamps and the warning to cross the line by foot-bridge. The gates were removed in October 1975 when lifting barriers were installed and the signalbox was dismantled later. The two old houses shown in this picture of 1905 and the wooden shops in front were pulled down in 1971.

48. Left: Stonelaying Ceremony, 26th June 1901, at the building of the new Congregational Church in Vernon Road, built by R. T. Hughes and Company at a cost of £3,883 (Vernon Halls were added in 1913) and opened 4th March 1902. The Stones laid commemorated the founding of the Church in 1662, the Sunday School Centenary in 1897, and John Doulton, Junior. Note the inquisitive postman and his strange headwear; also, in the distance, the first council houses (or 'workmen's dwellings' as they were then called) being built in Alexandra Road by Barnes Urban District Council.

49. Below: William's Cottages built as the second Chapel of Mortlake Independent Church in 1802 at the corner of what is now St Leonards Road and Sheen Lane. Converted in 1836 into cottages by William (hence their name) Pocock, market gardener and member of the Church, who received the building in return for putting up the purchase moneys of £150 to enable the Church to acquire the copyhold of their first Chapel, built 1716 (and still standing at the corner of South Worple Way and Sheen Lane) which fell into other hands in 1755.

50. Left: Mud Cottages in Sheen Lane adjoined Williams Place, at the corner of St. Leonard's Road. Here they are shown in a very derelict condition prior to their demolition in 1903. Mr. Joseph Newman, the caretaker of the Limes (formerly the Council House in Mortlake High Street) stands here providing a great contrast in his well groomed bowler hatted apparel.

51. Below: Coronation Day, June 22nd, 1911. The clergy with the Borough of Islington Military Band leading the school children of Mortlake and East Sheen up Sheen Lane to Sheen House, there to sing the national anthem at 2 p.m., then to enjoy sports, amusements and tea until 6 o'clock. Parents and public were admitted at 5.30 p.m. for sports for those of 14-18 years from 7-9 p.m: dance music by the band until 11 p.m. The parishioners of Barnes enjoyed the same programme at The Priory with, of course, another band.

EAST SHEEN

52. **Left:** Milestone Green, East Sheen. A north-east view showing the milestone which still remains. The Green used to be much larger with no road on the east side and further land on the east and south-east which was taken into the grounds of The Larches and Sheen House. Boys used it as a cricket pitch, men for quoits, and on 5th November great bonfires were lit there. In 1859 Mortlake Green was acquired as a playground and a proper cricket pitch made there.

53. **Below:** The Triangle, East Sheen. The Triangle was the address of the few buildings in Sheen Lane at the south-east junction with the upper Richmond Road, after land was taken from the eastern side of Milestone Green to make a road and the Green became triangular in shape. An early '73 'bus can be seen, this being a turning point for 'buses at one time.

54. **Left:** A minor calamity in the Upper Richmond Road at the corner of The Triangle in East Sheen. The rear wheels of this steam wagon, owned by the Associated Portland Cement Manufacturers, have collapsed under the heavy load. The back is already jacked up with timber baulks. J. Clarke and Sons' dairy (later Hornby and Clarke) is new and the ivy clad house and Rose Cottage beyond are due for demolition, Broadway Buildings going up there in 1923. On the extreme left the shops east of Richmond Park Road await occupants.

55. **Below:** Juxon's Almshouses, East Sheen. This charity dates from 1626 but these almshouses appear to have been built in 1746 and were facing on to Church Path close to the Upper Richmond Road. Obviously there were four doors originally, so presumably four dwellings were later made into two. These were demolished in 1911 and on the site three almshouses were built facing in the opposite direction so that their frontages are in Milton Road.

Upper Richmond Road, East Sheen

56. **Left:** Prior to 1914 there was certainly no need for zebra crossings, as this picture looking east along the Upper Richmond Road clearly shows. Although the upper stories of the shops have changed little, the street lamps, hand carts and uncovered topped bus are clear reminders of an earlier and more leisured existence.

58. Below: In the early part of the twentieth century the Sheen branch of the Ministering Children's League raised money for a variety of good causes. Here is the cast of the Dick Whittington pantomine in the garden of Cricklewood, the home of the Misses Keller who organised the enterprise. This house formerly stood on the site now covered by the Prospect Telephone Exchange in the Upper Richmond Road. The part of Dick Whittington was played by Evelyn Leveaux with a charming supporting cast.

57. Above: Upper Richmond Road. The more charming aspect of 'The Hare and Hounds' in the early years of this century. The proprietor was advertising billiards, a bowling green, ping pong tables, a dining saloon, polo stables and other good stabling. The original date of the inn is unknown but it was 'The Hare and Hounds' in 1776. When 'Palewell' was sold in 1798 the sale particulars stated 'a pack of harriers is kept in the neighbourhood' and this could account for the name of the inn.

59. Left: A remnant of old East Sheen in 1930. These are Five Alls Cottages between Penrhyn Crescent and Sheen Gate Gardens, pulled down in 1934 to make way for shops. The odd name is from the cottage lying back by the tree on the right of the picture, a former beerhouse of that sign: being a clergyman, I pray for all; barrister, I plead for all; farmer, I maintain all; the King, I fight for all; and His Satanic Majesty, I take all. Beyond the tree are Aston Cottage and Geraldine Cottage.

These two photographs taken at the turn of the century are of considerable interest. **No. 60** shows Leinster Avenue under construction with Geraldine Villas in the Upper Richmond Road beyond.

No. 61 is practically a continuation. In the foreground is the site of Connaught Avenue. St. Anne's, on the left hand side of the picture, stood at the corner of Blind Lane (now Temple Sheen Road). This in turn led to Barker's nurseries which were later built over as Medcroft Gardens and Coval Road. In the distance Christ Church and Temple Sheen Villas can be clearly picked out. It is hard to realise that the hedged and fenced road running from east to west is now lined with shops and daily blocked with buses and juggernauts.

62.   Above: Pocock's Farm or Orchard Cottage. This farmhouse, viewed from the south, stood backing on to No. 611, Upper Richmond Road, between Berwyn Avenue and Sheen Common Drive. Here, in 1932, it is shortly to be demolished and the building material for houses in Orchard Drive is already stacked in position. The farm had been a market garden owned by Mr. Charlie Barker. (see No. 51 *Barnes. and Mortlake As It Was*).

63.   Right: The Sheen Kinema in the winter of 1938, a cheap and comfortable haven from the cold and the rumours of war, with Jack Buchanan in 'Break the News'. Owned by Joseph Mears, it replaced the Picturedrome, (see photograph 53), opened on Boxing Day 1910. With glowing neon it was renowned as an example of 'night architecture'. Inside was a theatre organ and a shifting prismatic lighting system with 672 permutations. It opened in December 1930. Later The Empire, it closed as the Sheen Odeon in June 1961, Parkway House taking its place at The Triangle.

64.   Above: This photograph of the garden front of the Cedars was taken on a hot summer afternoon when those attending a garden fete were glad to seek shade under sunshades or umbrellas. In the nineteenth and early twentieth centuries this was the home of the Leycester Penrhyn family who were connected through marriage with the Earls of Derby. The architecture of the house shows a variety of styles. It was demolished c.1930 and Cedar Court and Penrhyn Crescent built on the grounds.

65. **Left:** Sheen Lane. Looking north from a point near Palmerston Road in 1911, with the wall of Sheen House estate on the right and the entrance to 'The Firs' on the left. This photograph was taken by Mr. A. E. Flood who died at the age of 100 in 1979.

66. **Left:** In the early summer of 1900 the Automobile Club entertained the chief constables of counties to luncheon at Sheen House Club, Sheen Lane. In addition to hospitality the guests were driven round Richmond Park and later asked to state their views on the motor car as a factor in public transport. Judging from the present day situation in the Upper Richmond Road their reply was favourable.

67.   **Above:** Temple Grove School 1892. This famous East Sheen school prepared pupils for all public schools, but chiefly Eton and Harrow. The grounds were extensive and after the house was demolished in 1908 the chapel (left of the picture) was used by Mortlake Parish for youth work. It then stood in Palmerston Road until destroyed by enemy action in World War II. The pronounced dip in Observatory Road marks the former site of the lake which was a feature of Temple Grove estate.

68. **Below:** Sheen Mount, West Temple Sheen, was frequently in demand for garden fetes such as this one in aid of Church funds. There was plenty of room in the spacious grounds for teas and stalls. This is a south west view of the house on a summer afternoon between the two world wars. The house has now been demolished and Sheen Mount Primary School occupies the site.

69. Above Right: Fife Road. The entrance to Sheen Common as it was in the early years of this century. The triangular piece of ground, which to-day is covered with trees and shrubs, was at one time part of the pound where stray animals were taken to await their owners' claims.

70. **Below Right:** East Sheen Gate, Richmond Park. The approach to Richmond Park early in this century. The buildings on the left are part of the Clare Lawn estate.

71, 72. **Above and Left:** This is Sheen Lodge alias Sheen Cottage in 1903, eleven years after the passing of Professor Richard Owen (later knighted) who came there in 1852. It stood against the wall of Richmond Park inside Mortlake parish near East Sheen Gate and overlooked Adam's Pond, later renamed after the professor. The pretty thatched and many gabled place was damaged beyond repair in the last war and the fine garden was grubbed up. During the residence of the professor the famous visitors included Tennyson the poet, the composer Spohr, and Dickens, who enjoyed Mrs. Owen's homemade cream a treat. The impressive library in the study, also shown here, befitted the professor who was a distinguished scientist and director of the Natural History Museum, Kensington. It was through these windows that he may have watched Mortlake shrew-mothers at dawn and sunset uttering secret verses to cure infants of malaises and protect them from bewitching at the notorious shrew ash (see *No. 65 Barnes and Mortlake As It Was*) between his house and Sheen Cross Wood, the scion of which sturdily flourishes today.

73. **Above:** Lavender Girls, in common with the muffin man, the boiled shrimp and winkle man, the cats' meat man, and the gaslamp lighter, are now fast fading Mortlake memories. The two seen here belong to the days when the brewery and market gardens provided most of the living for the natives and innumerable lodgers. Lavender growing was a famous Surrey industry, notably around Mitcham.

74. **Above:** This Italian organ grinder, at one time complete with red-capped monkey, played on his regular days, between the two world wars, around the roads of the area. The tunes on his barrel were limited and despite his nationality, the best known in his repertoire was the Marseillaise. Daily he pushed his barrow to and from Hammersmith in all weathers and at all seasons. He regarded his 'musica' as his 'work' and it was of great importance to him as he helped people by cheering them up.